Salamanders Are Gross!

Leigh Rockwood

PowerKiDS press

New York

Published in 2011 by The Rosen Publishing Group, Inc.
29 East 21st Street, New York, NY 10010

First Edition

Editor: Maggie Murphy
Book Design: Ashley Burrell
Photo Researcher: Jessica Gerweck

Photo Credits: Cover, pp. 4, 5, 6, 8, 10, 21, 22 Shutterstock.com; pp. 7, 12, 13 (bottom left) George Grall/ Getty Images; p. 9 © www.iStockphoto.com/Armin Hinterwirth; p. 11 © www.iStockphoto.com/Lorenzo Rossi; p. 13 (top) © www.iStockphoto.com/Kevin Snair; p. 13 (bottom right) © www.iStockphoto.com/Mark Kostich; pp. 14—15 © www.iStockphoto.com/Ziva K.; p. 16 Gary Meszaros/Getty Images; p. 17 Marty Cordano/ Getty Images; p. 18 Gerold and Cynthia Merker/Getty Images; p. 19 Parke H. John Jr./Getty Images; p. 20 © www.iStockphoto.com/Stanislav Hulita.

Library of Congress Cataloging-in-Publication Data

Rockwood, Leigh.
  Salamanders are gross! / Leigh Rockwood. — 1st ed.
     p. cm. — (Creepy crawlies)
  Includes index.
  ISBN 978-1-4488-0702-4 (library binding) — ISBN 978-1-4488-1365-0 (pbk.) —
ISBN 978-1-4488-1366-7 (6-pack)
  1. Salamanders—Juvenile literature. I. Title.
  QL668.C2C54 2011
  597.8'5—dc22
                                          2010009115

Manufactured in the United States of America

CPSIA Compliance Information: Batch #WS10PK: For Further Information contact Rosen Publishing, New York, New York at 1-800-237-9932

Contents

The Slippery Salamander 4

A Double Life 6

The Salamander's Body..................8

Home, Wet Home........................ 10

Life Cycle 12

Fact Sheet: Gross! 14

What's for Dinner?..................... 16

The Tiger Salamander 18

The Fire Salamander 20

Shy and Slimy 22

Glossary 23

Index 24

Web Sites................................ 24

The Slippery Salamander

Salamanders are **amphibians** found in North America, South America, Asia, Europe, and northern Africa. Salamanders and lizards have similar body shapes. However, salamanders have soft, slimy skin like that of other amphibians, such

▼ Newts, such as this California newt, are one kind of salamander. There are many kinds of salamanders!

Salamanders are the family of amphibians that have tails as adults.

as frogs. Many salamanders live near bodies of freshwater because they need to keep their skin wet. They sleep in shady places during the day and spend their nights hunting for bugs and worms.

Did you know that if another animal catches a salamander by its tail, the salamander can make its tail fall off so that it can run away? Then, the salamander can **regenerate** its lost tail!

A Double Life

Amphibians, such as salamanders, live double lives. When they are first born, amphibians live in water and breathe using **gills**. Once they reach adulthood, many amphibians live on land and breathe using lungs.

Most salamanders are pretty small. They are generally between 3 and 8 inches (8–20 cm) long from head to tail.

Salamanders can be many different colors. Some salamanders are brightly colored, such as this black and yellow fire salamander!

This is a young red-spotted newt. At this point in its life, the newt lives underwater and breathes through gills.

Salamanders are the only amphibians that have tails throughout all periods of their lives. Other amphibians, such as frogs and toads, have tails that get smaller as they grow. They have disappeared totally once they reach adulthood. There are about 400 different **species** of salamanders in the world.

The Salamander's Body

Most salamanders have four legs and smooth, wet skin. This makes them look like a cross between a frog and a lizard. Like other amphibians, most salamanders breathe through lungs instead of gills when they are adults. However, some salamanders, such as mudpuppies, breathe through gills even as adults. This is because they live in

This marbled salamander has dirt sticking to its wet skin!

The axolotl is another kind of salamander that lives underwater its whole life. However, there are very few axolotls left in the wild.

water their whole lives. Their gills are on the sides of their heads.

There are species of salamanders that are very small and species that are really big. Minute salamanders are only about 1.5 inches (4 cm) long. Chinese giant salamanders grow up to 5.5 feet (2 m) in length and weigh around 140 pounds (63.5 kg).

Some salamander species, such as sirens and olms, live in water their whole lives. Adults of other species live on land in **habitats** that let them keep their skin wet and cool. Some, such as the tiger salamander, live in burrows they dig in the ground. Others, such as the spotted salamander, sleep under wet stones and logs.

This northern red salamander is staying cool in a pile of wet leaves.

Even salamanders that live mainly on land like to stay near water. Here, a salamander pokes its head out of a freshwater pond.

People are the biggest danger to salamander habitats both in water and on land. **Pollution** can hurt the land, air, or water that these animals need. People also build homes and roads in salamander habitats. This changes the habitat and leaves salamanders with fewer places to live. Some species, such as the California tiger salamander, have even become **endangered** because of habitat loss.

Life Cycle

2

When these salamanders reach adulthood, they live on land. Most salamanders **mate** in the early spring. Males try to draw females to them by waving their tails. If the female likes what she sees, she waves her tail to tell the male she wants to mate.

1

Land-dwelling salamanders hatch from eggs as **larvae**. First, they live in the water and breathe using gills. As the larvae get older, they grow legs and lungs.

As adults, some salamanders travel miles (km) away from the pond or stream where they were born. When it is time to mate, these salamanders go back to the place where they were born to lay their own eggs.

After the female's eggs are **fertilized** by the male, she lays hundreds of eggs in the water. The eggs are covered with poisonous matter to keep them safe. Larvae hatch from the eggs 19 to 50 days later.

3

Gross!

1 As salamanders grow, they shed their skin. Their shed skin does not go to waste, though, because the salamander then eats it!

2 Some salamanders can regenerate other body parts besides their tails. Some species can regenerate legs, eyes, or body organs!

3 Some salamanders are commonly called newts. Other salamanders are called axolotls, spring lizards, water dogs, or tritons.

4 Sirens are a type of salamander that has only two small front legs and no back legs. They use their tails to help them move in the water and in mud.

Algae grow on salamander eggs. The algae do not hurt the eggs. In fact, they help supply the eggs with oxygen, which helps them produce healthy larvae.

5

When a salamander regenerates a new tail, the new part is lighter in color than the rest of its body. Over time, the tail will darken to be the same color as the rest of the body.

6

There are species of salamanders that live in trees. Some of them have tails that can hold on to things like tree branches.

7

Some salamanders, such as the paddle-tail newt, have webbed toes.

8

What's for Dinner?

The first thing a salamander does when it comes out at night is start to look for food. Salamanders hunt using their sticky tongues. What do salamanders eat? Their food includes animals such as slugs, snails, worms, spiders, and bugs.

▼ Here, an adult red-spotted newt catches a young damselfly under water.

▶ This tiger salamander is snacking on an earthworm.

Most salamanders are small and slow moving. This makes some **predators**, such as skunks, turtles, owls, and snakes, look at them as tasty snacks. Some animals, though, see the salamander's brightly colored spots and know to stay away! This is because many salamander species let out a bad-tasting, poisonous liquid through their skin. The liquid gives the salamander a chance to get away.

The Tiger Salamander

Tiger salamanders are named for the brown and yellow stripes on their bodies. They remind some people of a tiger's stripes. These salamanders live in burrows near ponds, lakes, and streams. At 7 to 14 inches (18–36 cm) from head to tail, tiger salamanders are the largest land salamanders in North America. Like other salamanders, this species

Tiger salamanders, such as this Arizona tiger salamander, can be found all over North America.

In the wild, tiger salamanders like to live by ponds and slow-moving streams.

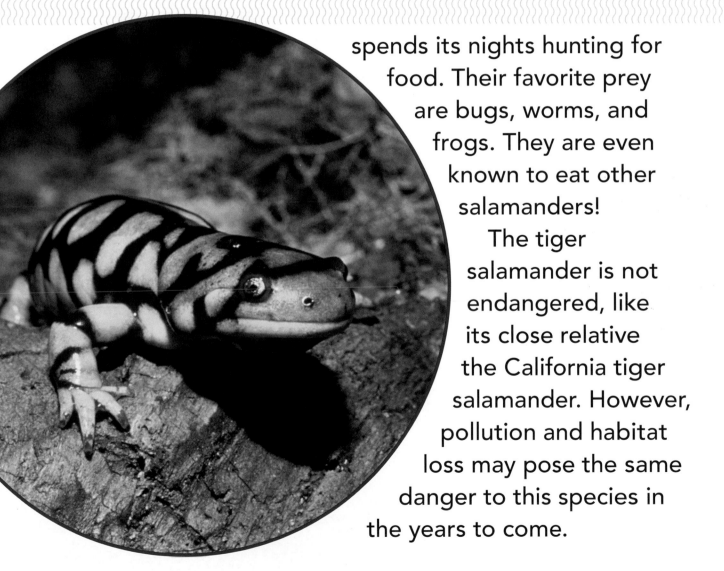

spends its nights hunting for food. Their favorite prey are bugs, worms, and frogs. They are even known to eat other salamanders!

The tiger salamander is not endangered, like its close relative the California tiger salamander. However, pollution and habitat loss may pose the same danger to this species in the years to come.

The Fire Salamander

The fire salamander is Europe's most commonly found salamander species. It is black with yellow spots. The fire salamander's name comes from the fact that people used to think that the animal could survive in fire. The truth is that often these salamanders were resting in logs being added to

▼ Adult fire salamanders are generally between 5 and 12 inches (13–30 cm) long.

Unlike most other salamanders, fire salamanders give birth to live larvae instead of eggs.

fires. Then, they ran out of the fires trying to get away from the flames!

The fire salamander has a lot of tricks to keep itself safe. Like other salamanders, it can let out a bad-tasting, poisonous matter through its skin. In addition, the fire salamander has poison **glands** near its eyes. If another animal gets too close, the salamander can spray poison into the eyes or mouth of the animal to scare it away!

Shy and Slimy

Salamanders are shy animals. They spend a great deal of time on the lookout for and hiding from people and other animals. Many species also **hibernate** for months at a time to get out of cold weather. These species do this because salamanders are cold-blooded.

Being cold-blooded means that salamanders' body temperatures change with the temperature around them.

Some people keep salamanders as pets. The tiger salamander is the species most commonly kept as a pet. It is not a cuddly pet, however. The salamander's skin is easily hurt. It also lets out a poisonous liquid that can hurt a person's skin. People who own salamanders enjoy watching these shy but fascinating pets.

Glossary

algae (AL-jee) Plantlike living things without roots or stems that live in water.

amphibians (am-FIH-bee-unz) Animals that spend the first part of their lives in water and the rest on land.

endangered (in-DAYN-jerd) In danger of no longer living.

fertilized (FUR-tuh-lyzd) To have eggs that are growing into babies.

gills (GILZ) Body parts that are used for breathing in the water.

glands (GLANDZ) Organs or parts of the body that produce something that helps with a bodily function.

habitats (HA-buh-tats) The kinds of land where animals or plants naturally live.

hibernate (HY-bur-nayt) To spend the winter in a sleeplike state.

larvae (LAHR-vee) Animals in the early period of life in which they have a wormlike form.

mate (MAYT) To come together to make babies.

pollution (puh-LOO-shun) Manmade wastes that hurt Earth's air, land, or water.

predators (PREH-duh-terz) Animals that kill other animals for food.

regenerate (rih-JEH-nuh-rayt) To grow or produce something again.

species (SPEE-sheez) One kind of living thing. All people are one species.

Index

A
amphibians, 4, 6–8

B
bugs, 5, 16, 19

E
eggs, 12–13, 15

F
freshwater, 5

G
gills, 6, 8–9, 12
glands, 21

H
habitat loss, 11, 19
habitat(s), 10–11

L
larvae, 12–13, 15
lizard(s), 4, 8, 14

N
night(s), 5, 16, 19
North America, 4, 18

P
pollution, 11, 19
predators, 17

S
skin, 4–5, 8, 10, 14,
   17, 21–22
South America, 4
species, 7, 9–11,
   14–15, 17–20, 22
spring, 12

T
tail(s), 5–7, 12, 14–15,
   18

W
weather, 22
worms, 5, 16, 19

Web Sites

Due to the changing nature of Internet links, PowerKids Press has developed an online list of Web sites related to the subject of this book. This site is updated regularly. Please use this link to access the list:
www.powerkidslinks.com/creep/mander/